Step 1
Go to **www.openlightbox.com**

Step 2
Enter this unique code

NVJHW4AMX

Step 3
Explore your interactive eBook!

Your interactive eBook comes with...

Golden Retriever

Start!

Share

AV2 is optimized for use on any device

 Read
Audio
Listen to the entire book read aloud

 Videos
Watch informative video clips

 Weblinks
Gain additional information for research

 Try This!
Complete activities and hands-on experiments

 Key Words
Study vocabulary, and complete a matching word activity

 Quizzes
Test your knowledge

 Slideshows
View images and captions

 Share
Share titles within your Learning Management System (LMS) or Library Circulation System

 Citation
Create bibliographical references following APA, CMOS, and MLA styles

This title is part of our AV2 digital subscription

1-Year K–2 Subscription
ISBN 978-1-7911-3310-8

Access hundreds of AV2 titles with our digital subscription.
Sign up for a FREE trial at **www.openlightbox.com/trial**

The digital components of this book are guaranteed to stay active for at least five years from the date of publication.

Golden Retriever

CONTENTS

2 Interactive eBook Code
4 Clever and Loving
6 Medium-Sized Dogs
8 Coat Colors
10 Growing Up
12 Family Dogs
14 Exercise
16 Grooming
18 Food and Attention
20 Staying Healthy
22 Incredible Golden Retrievers
24 Sight Words

My golden retriever is clever and loving.

She is friendly with new people.

Golden retrievers are medium-sized dogs. They are strong, sturdy, and athletic.

Dog Shoulder Heights

English Cocker Spaniel
Up to 17 inches
(43 centimeters)

Golden Retriever
Up to 24 inches
(61 cm)

Labrador Retriever
Up to 24.5 inches
(62 cm)

Golden retrievers have thick, golden coats.

They can be light or dark shades of gold.

Most golden retriever puppies have light coats.

As they grow, their coats often become darker.

Where in the World

Golden retrievers were first bred in Scotland in the 1800s. Scotland is a country in the United Kingdom.

Golden retrievers make good family pets.

Most enjoy being around people. They are gentle with children.

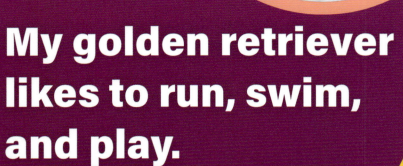

My golden retriever likes to run, swim, and play.

I take her for long walks every day.

She is happy to play fetch on land or in water.

My golden retriever's fur is long and fluffy. I brush her often.

She sheds her coat one or two times a year.

I feed my golden retriever twice a day.

We spend time together. She loves attention from our family.

I take my golden retriever to the veterinarian at least once a year.

The veterinarian helps keep my dog healthy.

Dog Breed Popularity in the United States

#1 French Bulldog

#2 Labrador Retriever

#3 Golden Retriever

A female golden retriever will have about **4** to **12 puppies** in a litter.

Golden retrievers were originally bred to **help hunters.** They can be trained to retrieve, or fetch, birds.

SIGHT WORDS

Research has shown that as much as 65 percent of all written material published in English is made up of 300 words. These 300 words cannot be taught using pictures or learned by sounding them out. They must be recognized by sight. This book contains 63 common sight words to help young readers improve their reading fluency and comprehension. This book also teaches young readers several important content words, such as proper nouns. These words are paired with pictures to aid in learning and improve understanding.

Page	Sight Words First Appearance
4	and, is, my, new, people, she, with
6	are, they, to, up
9	be, can, have, light, of, or
10	most
11	a, as, country, first, grow, in, often, the, their, were, where, world
12	around, being, children, family, good, make
14	day, every, for, her, I, likes, long, play, run, take, walks
15	land, on, water
17	one, times, two, year
19	from, our, together, we
20	at, helps, keep, once, states

Page	Content Words First Appearance
4	golden retriever
6	dogs, English cocker spaniel, heights, Labrador retriever, shoulder
9	coats, gold, shades
10	puppies
11	Scotland, United Kingdom
12	pets
15	fetch
17	fur
19	attention
20	breed, French bulldog, popularity, United States, veterinarian

Published by Lightbox Learning Inc.
276 5th Avenue, Suite 704 #917
New York, NY 10001
Website: www.openlightbox.com

Copyright ©2026 Lightbox Learning Inc.
All rights reserved. No part of this publication may be reproduced, stored in a retrieval system, or transmitted in any form or by any means, electronic, mechanical, photocopying, recording, or otherwise, without the prior written permission of the publisher.

Library of Congress Control Number: 2024057389

ISBN 979-8-8745-2158-5 (hardcover)
ISBN 979-8-8745-2159-2 (softcover)
ISBN 979-8-8745-2160-8 (static multi-user eBook)
ISBN 979-8-8745-2162-2 (interactive multi-user eBook)

012025
100924

Printed in Guangzhou, China
1 2 3 4 5 6 7 8 9 0 29 28 27 26 25

Project Coordinator: Priyanka Das
Designer: Jean Faye Rodriguez

Every reasonable effort has been made to trace ownership and to obtain permission to reprint copyright material. The publisher would be pleased to have any errors or omissions brought to its attention so that they may be corrected in subsequent printings.

The publisher acknowledges Getty Images and Shutterstock as its primary image suppliers for this title.